Common Time

Chris Pusateri

Paperback edition:
ISBN-10: 0983632626
ISBN-13: 978-0-9836326-2-7

Kindle edition:
ISBN-10: 0983632634
ISBN-13: 978-0-9836326-3-4

Cover design by HR Hegnauer.

Some of these poems originally appeared in *Zoland Poetry*, *Colorado Review*, *Eleven-Eleven*, *Mandorla* and *Action, Yes*.

Many thanks to Joe Amato, Jeremy Biles, Kass Fleisher and Michelle Naka Pierce.

~STEERAGE PRESS~
steeragepress.com
Boulder, Colorado and Normal, Illinois

[Contents]

the conch,   hears the ocean (31)   indicating
cold (32)   up, but (33)
            processing (34)
            dinner, when (35)

        from the clouds emerges a ship (36)
        The schoolboy asked for (37)

This message is
        for (38)   the many people who came briefly
        to rest in it. (39) in English, then shortly after,
switch (40)
flesh and its billions of hosts (41)
it's clear, even from a distance, (42) there's no
peace (43)

When we are through, (44)
this simple matter of stripping away (45)   'the lesser
of two,' (46)

the precise heft of past matters (47) Everyone
        who wants (48) the calories
            it gives, (49)
        might scupper language (50)
                        they go round
                            endlessly (51) counting

                    Except that
                        The counting only goes (52)
freestanding or part of a larger (53) somewhere
deep (54)   what we utter. Within (55)

Through the vast cloud-cover (56) There are times
when you wonder (57)   The image freezes (58) and

would never be (59)

There is one
        and none (60)   fictions
        that happened (61) *I don't know where* (62)

first is the story (63)   you do not know (64)
  as it takes shape (65)   through the shadow of
  all possibly (66)   In the Hopes (67)

You will run (68) but you won't (69)   miss,
something that (70)   could make   you smile
that way (71)   plotting,
the memory (72)
what we call
        ethnicity (73)
worry), recurring (74)   we wilt, growing rapid (75)
you need
another year's (76)
none will win (77)
nor half-full: the glass (78)

your avatar unincorporated (79)   outlet'
through which
    pedestrians (80)
for access, we use
users (81)   for this end time, for the passenger. (82)

I've always believed…that one should start by worrying about the action of the instrument, not the sound.
(Glenn Gould)

…and every *not* is a little blank space in the canvas, defined by the remains of an assertion.
(D. H. Lawrence)

But a gigantic adroit never aided,
      except as everyman
      Pluto expels impotence—I mean **droits
        and hinges** in fenestration
          on soothsayer baseboards
            totteling bongos

  Slowly remember then,
those tightlipped lilies,
      for what they are
         is smoking notes
         in the notion of a mighty idea

my drink rising
      into rain—

      the city's tense grey gait

I doubt an idea usually
as you raise your hand to use the john
& go to the cloakroom to pee.

while thy errand it journeyed on

an illuminated skyline
we remember color only

seatbacks of red leather
free wi-fi and it's warm

[movies are better than cinema]

We're getting settled
as the program begins

as the program begins
clouds disappear

two empty specimen cups
as I cross the street

as I cross the street
the siren expands

the siren expands
in other words: dead

in other words:
what makes a brain a mind?

a mind a brain made plural
a crowd of breathing t-shirts

[there's no accounting for memory]

One string
two notes
tin cans **on either
end.**   **A moment**
    of silence pulled
    tighter—tried
 same words,
 different string

Misprision doorman memorial
'same old tinsel as last Christmas'

from links **bent together meant to**
keep things to either side of it

, a cigarette's whisper

that smells like something misspelled
non-normative but phonetically tight

, to each constituent her chain

of events, vivacious as orange

for aspirin as these names are restored

'same old tinsel as last Christmas'

in the pen is poems or memos
  depending

Dust been skin and having been will again.

Keys in brief,
        shifting in
                measure. Springs
dither, silver miller, broad strokes
    tamed in manger. My head unbettered. My sight
misreckoned.

                        They will **never say**
                        never again. Bluff once and
            peter. Bluff twice and shrink.

My gifts are Priam; my rubbers are expired; my discs
are loaded; my sighs are hired.

    Ply eyes
        with what can't be seen.
Fuck nature's favors
and pine
for something plastic, will I. We'll cotton once,
scolding heat from Hermes' feet. We
                                will
                                    do you
                                one
                                    better

                            than yours
                        does
                            you.

Take 1

On one hand
: *she*. On the other:
what
   refers to, but
does not touch.

Disembodied plurality refracts its contrary.

Therefore, in one hand: a wish.
In the other: the ungiven.

Take 2

Bathed in despair, she sought water.
On one hand, she wanted
   rid of what
      the other hand referred to.

(we *could* care less, of only some **if, conditions** fixed
                              if, should agency
                              & chance coalesce).

                     Peel & strip. When it
                  screams, it's admissible.

                  Anything it utters
                        may be presumed

true: no tracks for those ahead. Those kingdoms of
severed residence, floating in a fine lidless galleon.
The filaments of a sob gone south.

(eyes suffering the great wrong of television

Everyone loves
  peace & has ideas
    about its kingdom on earth.

Of only some *if,* conditions
fixed *if,* should agency
& chance
  coalesce, then.

[There's no accounting for memory]

We're getting settled
        as the program begins

Time to clean
Assorted papers
Assorted words
This is it
Time to clean

Man as legend
Unreached by razor
Yours is New York
So brutally smooth

Song going round
Words, numbers
Signs of luck
In jeans, preening

Paradox rises from the rose

An ethics, **voluminous**
The siren expands
Watched, never boils
In other words: dead

Daimler, Dear

Dear Daimler, your bather is too far off to come of
                                        much
Dear Daimler, there is nothing I wouldn't do
Dear Daimler, the wind invites and the wind
                                        impedes
Dear Daimler, fire reminds us
Dear Daimler, it is visible and oriented north
Dear Daimler, the light is growing old, takes refuge
Dear Daimler, it's habit and I'll cleave
Dear Daimler, unique means 'for sale'
Dear Daimler, you are mass-produced, embraceable
Dear Daimler, I am encumbered, enamored of
Dear Daimler, open drapery gives permission
Dear Daimler, disaster relief is bum comfort
Dear Daimler, 'fuck' is an everyday low price
Dear Daimler, you can't roll if you're square
Dear Daimler, friends, sorted by relevance
Dear Daimler, an open envelope with cancelled
                                        stamp
Dear Daimler, the naked breeze of a fresh haircut
Dear Daimler, your means are sound advice
Dear Daimler, the comma is foreplay
Dear Daimler, stubble **is taxation**
Dear Daimler, suitcases, our better angels
Dear Daimler, with all the beauty of a spoon
Dear Daimler, just one mile more

The lime green of evening even
  taxes (the afterlife) the very water
              it autumned

  & a belt to hold it up with

a strange rust spreading
                  from the ceiling tells no tiles
                  but I reassure it **that**
                      one needs not begin

& that exploratory metaphysics is the sum total of
all experiments. Even email.

There is Irish & malt; there are bookmarks and
endpapers. We'll mark a place, we'll never return.

I want to know
the difference between
my expectations and reality,
and I want to know why
when they fight,
one always wins.

It's like a flow chart where everything flows
sideways. A 'flat hierarchy' says the boss at the
plant.

You are currently using 17.9 percent of your ability.
The amount increases when you sleep.

Most take it where they can get it. Human misery is
a product of not knowing what *it* is.

It is an hourglass without sand.
You will say this is abstract language.
That you are 'over it.'

Everyone loves peace
and has ideas.

(A prison tattoo signifying affiliation)

Your civic duties depend upon which community
you belong to.

Mao is now friends with Madame Chiang; Ashlee is
now friends with Ashlee.

This profile has been viewed 538 times.

We could go back to
drafts, revise slightly,
but there would always be
the forward thinking, the furniture
we'd tethered the future
to, to
antedate
our intentions, so that
even prescience
would seem passé.

Each thing being metaphor,
"you" are not the 'you' I met effortlessly over
breakfast, *you*
is a word that yields
to some other symptom of significance.

You might say *fraud*, your hands rich with printer's
ink,
your forearms forming X, an article of effacement
in an answer that does not insist, yet set
in parliamentary distinction, chic flue a
sidewise of something subsequent,
the plum dust of wonder
never feels itself settle.

Nostalgia **is mortal and completes** us
before we are ready.

Mnemonics its somber prerogative,
promise like sovereigns divested of red
sputter, bodiless
like pods to the bottom.

Always take a grey suit, so you'll be ready
for anything, says William Hurt. Grey
the color of rain, a necessary evil,
is the color of alloy, of shale. A tintype
of mama, an uncle's disposition: it's the stuff
documentaries are made of.

> Hold the chair, hold
> the door. When you can't know what,
> say 'sometimes.'

When all else fails, enjamb
like a fetus, curl to circles,
  live like everything
  worth noticing
  takes place
    on your lap.

I'll cry so you can hear me. It's a language
of flight that wants not
to run. There will be a corner
of the house where **things accumulate
and this** will be a sign of good fortune.

However.

The remainder will be breathed
  elliptically, where the meaning's in the tone,
not the message.

It's the literal world you're worrying over.

It's not that we like each other,
but it's not that we don't.

(That's a binary in search of a glory hole).

Give the pet what fell from the table.

Just because it's a disposal doesn't mean you can
feed it anything.

There **is something mutterable**
about the way
the light picks on the empty glass.

Its fixings are the sad yaks of matter.

People wouldn't understand,
    but a person might.

i.

Unfortunately, there's no cheat sheet for **living.**
Your investment in life
is in line with
your tolerance for risk. It might seem
like it's your choice, but it
is. Does the double positive
nullify itself or is its
affirmative power cumulative?

So very, very.

ii.

If you have to ask
'are you kidding me?'
then, no, they're in earnest
about whatever absurd thing
they want you to believe.

iii.

There will be pain, but it will be someone else's
until it's not,
and then it is again. Then it becomes
empathy, a virtue.

If you compile enough virtues,
you can trade them for sainthood,
although a saint to whom
is a question that remains unbaked
but is always just below the icing,
like sugary rot.

The low voices trick us
with their volume, into believing
  against belief, forgetting
  what we know this place to be.

I don't want to give him my books because I don't
think he reads
  but how's he supposed to read
if no one ever thinks he will?

Okay, seven percent, but seven percent of what?

The distance that separates us **is greater now
  than ten** years ago
  even though we live in the same places.

My message is so long, it has become a religious
text.

To read it is to be not informed, but devoted.

Strapless mocha. Steaming penis fondue.

As you age, your vocabulary shrinks
even as your grasp of grammar grows.

There is a feeling
that you've put something
where it doesn't belong.

You sitting in this armchair
is like an almond
remembering it tastes like cyanide.

There is something
we say in moments like these.
It is short, monosyllabic,
and does not end in an upsweep.

Because you're red, people think
you're a drinker, when actually
you're a runner.

Recalibrated claw sliding and yet had changed and
Somehow
Put his other kiss to her
Finally he pulled it off
She was worried something terrible had happened

You *are* conditional
His gaze, again, **moving**
Shouted with her blouse
His gaze, again, **moving**

What scratchily he is, drunk
And me, sometimes,
Dark flannel gave the thumbs
Visible, opposable, signal
Meant what it meant
Whatever: that

You'll finally put on
A year, a little, perhaps
Mean who she
Loves already half-vanished
In steaming penis fondue
Expressionless entryway without yolk

The more it's made the less we force the issue
Playful teeth were for an instant
Clothes frustrated, bad choice encumbered
Which he hadn't seen, but waited, explained

Tax my cowardice until I'm nothing but an x-ray
                                                negative.

Only when I abandon ethics, do I become
                the inventor I might be? And that's only
                about twenty minutes a day. I can
retroactively activate my ethics
                by erasing the text
                I wrote during the forty minutes
                a day when I was twice the inventor but
half the man I was born to be.

                        I think all
                    sentences
                    should end in
                        infinitives. It lends
                    this whole nasty enterprise a note
                of hope, like
                    leaving one window of your home
                        unboarded
                    as the hurricane approaches.

Chimes are time's way of reminding you
to worry. Like time
  telling the story of itself; is how we
  pluralize memory—
by planting notions in the heads of the young
  until they're sure they remember
  the conditions of their births.

What we desire
in manuscript
is not what
we value
in life:

a sameness, a consistency smooth as the movies.

When cleaning up
  someone else's mess, you discover
    some small secrets. **For instance, an instant**
when the child wouldn't stop crying and his dad hid
him under a pile of fresh laundry, thinking
the scent of flowers would calm him.

    That night had a weave
unlike any past fabric.
        We know these phrases and keep
repeating them.

You can't hate people when you see them sleeping,
but you can hate what they dream.

Metered in the weight
  of its breaking,

    he felt his mind

      shear

from its
  couplings—moments when

      we feel the friction of time
     grinding past, spending us
      perchance its fancy, the moment
    pulled from our chests
      like a bloody handkerchief.

If the study of literature has taught me
　　　　it's that there are no unsympathetic
characters—even **Hitler's mother**
　　　　　　　　kissed him on
　　　　　　　the cheek.

　　　　A slowing as the processor struggles to
　　　　digest the pasted HTML text.

When the clock strikes half,
　and not a ringtone before.

　　　　　In this once again
　　　　　　　lime green of evening,

　　　　　　the rusted wrench of eating,
　　　　　　the smack daddy of gabbing,
　　　　　　　the card dealt
　　　　　　　　and let with
　　　　　　　　　your last bottom
　　　　　　　　　sawbuck,

　　　(put me down for five)

we pack our last batter into the box
　　　　　and holler 'hey'.

A penny saved.

Watch as it disappears into economic indicators.

If you think nature is innocent, then it's never tried
to kill you.

His love of statistics
is not a love of numbers
but a love of the concepts
those numbers represent:
    the proclivities
  and tendencies
      of how we figure.

There is a green
in the picture
that is no natural
  chemical process,

    so we think to ourselves
      that such a place
        could never exist.

      A possibility is but a causeway
      that joins two
      prospects into a single
      maybe.

I had this idea
that if I sat in one place
for a very long time without moving

and was **very quiet,**

that I might
gradually
cease to exist.

There would be a pistol loaded with our dreams.
We would **enact a massacre** by shooting people
with those dreams, and like heroes in the movies,
our revolver would never run out of bullets.

    I ache in Maine, its green waters and tiny
whitecaps so unlike my deposits
      but the movement
      (perhaps the way I wish to move)
        might resemble
in tonnes the way the water
        shuffles toward shore
where it argues with itself
        before retreating.

Some things we cannot recognize as nutrients.

There are symbols & sheets and days made blank.

It's salt, residual.

Like licking the hand of a lover
  after it's been inside of you—

you learn something that way,
though you may not want it.

We would like information that supports our
ignorance.

You know: books where the fear's in the font.

The pen **is black but the ink** is blue: that's what's
meant by collusion.

You talk like a sergeant, but you fuck like a
milkman: that's what's meant by dissonance.

The irregular lowing
  of the moment
    reminds us that
      lucidity
        is a bovine fixation on a single instant.

There is a black phone with no one on it.

I'm staring at it intently: a listening kind of gaze
                          that fills everything.

Does writing create   a moment
                          or does it exist in a moment
  which it illuminates by drawing our attention to it?

When I press *discard*, what I really want is for
                          something better to appear.
But all I see is nothingness,
itself a presence,
awaiting a mate.

Nobody knows how long fifteen minutes really
takes.

Even the most creative of endeavors are
                             documentary,
if enough time passes.

The rising seas will make for great data models.

But models are not reality.

When drowning in orange,
reach for peaches: canned, halved, faintly tinny.

There's something of the earth in them.

The stench of self
        is so heavy today
        we feel like we're being lovingly caressed
by the movements of a million sympathetic reptiles.

Perhaps I crave something that offends my friends
because I see it as hostile to my own sensibilities.

        We'll drill into your skullplate, kiddo.

        The metal bit
          will invite bone
            to make way for
              its revolutionary rhetoric.

            The claim that all will yield
              to sufficient force,

          that we **can change all forms**
          because it was we who perceived them.

When the forms begin,
golemlike, to speak,
  we wish for the return of routine,

we will ask, plead, beg,
        and when necessary, kill
                for its return.

(**the conch**, where Gatsby **hears the ocean**)

When subtracting, you'll notice
      that arrears is a concept, not a real number.

        Sometimes, sleeping dogs
      resemble dead dogs.

The container had a blue lid,
    indicating cold fluid within.

'I write with my hands, not my heart'

I ordered the plot with a dram of
               mayonnaise,
    to thicken it.

I roasted tomatoes & made a sofa.

You think I'm hung **up, but** I'm processing…

34

<----------processing...

There was a time, at **dinner, when** her mother
                              asked if I was gay.

'But I'm dating your daughter,' I said.

But there's that pause again, the one that reminds us
at three removes, that nothing
can be explained, nothing
can be vicarious.

Beyond that strata
there can be only
fiction.

When seeking something,

we often encounter Aristotle's aphorism
in which our failure to achieve something

is a failure of will rather than something innate.

Like finding pot 'if I really wanted to, I could,'
when 'could' is a term
incongruous with the figure speaking it.

It was a shirt
that read 'travesty'
rather than being a travesty.

I'll be the judge of every Winnebago.

And **from the clouds emerges a ship**
from the ink which is
the tattoo which is the image
of something punted.

Rule number one in the city: you never
        just *throw* yourself down on a patch of grass.

The rubber band sits on the counter, fastening
nothing.

The schoolboy asked for a working definition
of postmodernism.

    A: If X is traveling toward his death at an ever-
       increasing pace (diet, exercise, and
       cholesterol drugs notwithstanding) then
       when will he converge with Y, if $Y=life$?

It is like running through tall corn,
a possibility unrealized as we roam.

This message is for whoever is unreachable at this time.

When I cup my hand, it signifies nothing.

I remember
the room,
its ancient paint
and **the many people
who came briefly to rest in it.**

Prolonged endurance of this condition is called
'training'

Washington DC (3)

There was a family at breakfast: man, woman,
genderless infant, and two young girls under ten.
The mother paused between sips of coffee to berate
the girls in French. The admonishments had to do
with food. She would ask them if they wanted more
to eat **in English, then shortly after, switch** to
French to chastise them for overeating.

Themselves is not other,
    are not a group of non-youses,
    but are, in fact, your **flesh and its billions**
    of hosts microbial.

Nothing (and the snacks it packs)
      has come to the zoo to pet the animals,
    who know him by the name 'extinction,'
    a friend whose acquaintance they're sure to make

is bliss of a different sort (for reasons repeatable,
but why?)

I am memorized by that
which is my antithesis.

Washington DC (1)

This hotel is
a Hollywood façade—beautiful landscaping
on a beautiful avenue,
    a mildly elegant first floor.

'Merlot is merlot!' screams the waitress
at the barkeep, as if truth were red.

Bananarama is on the juke,
and I'm sure the waitress would agree
        that Bananarama
        is Coltrane
        is Muddy Waters is
        Pavarotti is
        Black Flag.

And shit is mercy,
Democrats are Republicans
DC is Disneyland
& my ass is a hat.

All distinctions vanish.

There is a man in here
who looks like Ilya's genuine article,
and **it's clear, even from a distance,**
that to him
merlot is not just a cigar.

I wonder what kind of poem Jack Collom would
write about this place (& if he has)?

Sarah's chap says it well: I am 'at once a person & a
piece of furniture.'

War Poem

> Currently, **there's no peace**
> to keep.

What would it look like
> the morning after victory?

> Be suspicious
> of the many offensives
> > that occur during the drawdown.

Be suspicious of a way out; be suspicious
> of analogies.

'You can't win a war for your values
by undermining them,' he said.

And then he began to cry.

When we are through, we will be unforgiveable.

Perhaps we could get Donald Rumsfeld to do the
calculus.

*You go to the hereafter with the handicaps you have, not with
the handicaps you wish you had.*

And if we're speaking conditionally,
please stand ready
so we can have you stand down
before you rise again.

If in doubt, lend it no voice.
If it doesn't speak, then it can't be said to exist.

It's not that we wish
to disrespect the dead by calling them 'forces'
as in the phrase 'five US forces killed by roadside
bomb.' No. It's simply
that we wish they were born
without names, so that **this simple matter
of stripping away** their faces wouldn't strike
the stakeholders (again, a pig bank for numbers)
as crass or careless.

In the background I can hear a baby crying,
but then I shake my head
& it clears.

How about if
when I say 'forces,'
you shake your head at the same time,
so that certain parasitic sentiments
do not gain purchase.

They have rendered themselves voic'd
by subtracting everything minus one.

kill can when
free meters kill can free filler
when kill as kill can
this man, this killer
kills when he tells
can kill for the greater,
kill for the fact,
kill his killer before the killer can
unhand him when in
actuality the kilt is
the killer because this man, this killer,
dims our wits with filler.

talk bother mutter matter,
this is 'discourse,'
'the lesser of two,'
this arithmetic minus eyes, senses stilled,
knows only that
this is.

slower motor a matter for ratchets
a salvo sitting calmly in its quiver
awaiting word of the third of three.

uttered code, watch hand ever lower on the cipher.
some language base whose unsexed tongues
mother plums,
a line of pearls along the larynx.

pharyngeal access with passkey functionary
we polish the nouns
grace the nameplate,
an umbilicus swearword in the throat of
whatever generation proceeds from here.

There is no say
of waying, this way of
unsaying is
charnel chiseled
into the mist of its shivering.

We could no more stain than stay,
    when embrace takes into you something
of the other. There is no say of waying, yet

weight we will, **the precise heft
   of past matters**, some come to naught,
 others fallen to rot. There is no say.

There is no place like home,
an interesting axiom we'll leave to beaver.

Neither laughter nor happenstance nor bonny
striped bee.

Something will come along.

What it drags
behind will come naturally
and you will call it that
for no better reason than that
order is a form of rhetoric

and you have persuaded yourself
   that there is no other way of saying.

It is the simplicity of math—
numbers, sums,
they fuck like lilies

and spawn like carp.

So we don't know the status, or what
is the state of us.

What is bad is removed: editing.
What is bad is removed: delusion.

There is more to mortar
than holding things together.

When what is bad is removed: suicide.

It's about more than simply
changing the fixtures.

When what is bad is removed: neuter.

Utopia: **Everyone who wants** one, has one.
Capitalism: Everyone who wants one, wants one.

The letters look small,
  the paper thinner
  in the way soup
    is thinner, **the calories it gives**,

the tiny death it gives off,
in the way mosquitoes 'give off' malaria.

In layers on the quay, we speak of,
we speak, from whence we.

Fingers dragging in wet sand,
the lines in time carried away
as a coverlet is lifted, and in mind, replaced.

There is a hint   of black on his breast   that makes
him seem   somewhat less a robin   and
something more his own.

We can see why, lacking an answer,
one **might scupper language**
        in favor of something more gestural.

Putting the notes to sleep, said Art Tatum
   of the ballad. Think of low tempo
      as a form of local anesthetic. I can hear
         his cuffs on the keys, a metal almost tin,
            something imitative, some quiet mime.

      Trailing notes as object to shadow
      'no ideas but in things' made so by our presence,
                        our prescience.

Looking out the window
    on my way each day
      I discover things
        that were previously invisible:
          a funeral parlor,
          a pawnbroker,
          a sausage shop.

And then there are the people—

        the little moving fortresses
        of whom Thoreau so lovingly wrote.

Like the tines of a tyre, **they go round endlessly**,
    being vexed only when
    they are pulled like a bad tooth
        from the duration of their habits.

          You can tell from east.
          You can sun from bugger.

          You can turn on the blur,
            then add, baby, add.

I'm not doing this
       to embarrass or humiliate you.
       I'm not
doing this to amuse myself. I'm not
         doing this
       for the benefit of your politics
       or to satisfy your need to see me
          as an asshole iconoclast.

       I'm not for me,
       nor in it for you.

I'm within five weeks of the gold watch.
I'm one case of non-dairy creamer away
             from a pink Mary Kay Cadillac.

I'm suspended above stars, which you call ceiling.

I'm sick of my name; I'm sick of yours
         & you.

I'm thirty-nine and **counting. Except that
  the counting only goes** one way.

I'm not doing this
  for the vain illusion of eternal youth. I'm not
      doing this to save time
      or money. I'm
not doing this
for fame or prestige,
  for the love of the game or the thrill of the chase.

I'm not doing what you think I'm doing
which is nothing
if nothing is time and its extinction.

Are you **free-standing or part of a larger** project?

Like Richard Burton,
you will enjoy a renaissance,
a second coming.

From **somewhere deep** within the oblivion of
Andromeda,
you will note its approach. And you will smile,
without laughter.

To say something matters, is to watch
an abstraction harden
into something that can kill.

It reminds me—not
'of' something, but reminds me,
brings me back
from where I was, which was
far from cognition.

There is a grid within
   what we utter.
         Within phonemes, associations form
            and dissolve like flies on bison.

  Lifting only to settle,
briefly, within time.

And rising alive to drift.

Through the vast cloud-covered cabbage
that was Sugarloaf Mountain,
       we tasted grain and everything
       the wind had traveled through—

             every evergreen, every smokestack,
                 every act of osmosis—in—
          and out through the mouth,
                  in the structure
                 of language that
                 gives so little but
                 that little
                   is
                   meaning.

Rise 5am to see the thin film of mist over the lake's
surface.

The faint sound of a mouse in the wall, excavating
his way to heat.

There are times when you wonder if happiness
isn't just another form of melancholy.

A loan surfaces like a grey bruise.

In that part of the lake, there's no deep casting.

6am: Bill heads out in the canoe.
Mark rises,
pisses,
sleeps some more.

Someone in the other room is farting and snoring
simultaneously.

It's so quiet you can hear a cigarette burn.

As your shadow shifts
around the kitchen table,
this rude clapboard cabin
aligns itself against
the oncoming
orbital logic of winter.

There is rarely this kind of silence anymore.

Only during holidays or in the wake of a tornado,
                              when nothing exists as it did.

The green shirt gave weight to his slight frame.

But there's a purring in the chest of the calendar, a promise—

The image freezes congeals   fades for another
   to bleed over it and take its turn at the wheel.

Never will you appear. (And) never again shall I
                              appear for you.

There is something in the packaging
            that instills in me
            a feeling of trust I am
            instantly suspicious of
                        trust.

Taken together
there is a fifty percent chance
that at the moment of greatest need
I will forget the Spanish verb for 'to take'

and would never be
if I were then able
to subtract the greater space of fifty
from what remains.

Through the hole in your lip
they'll string you,
proof duplex, on one side
me.

Then there is your other fifty—your better half.

There is 5, 10,
15 & **one**;
and 12, 6,
16
and none.

I'll trade you one symbol for its equivalent,
so long as we agree
on their equivalence.

Autobiography = **fictions that happened** to me.

Interviews

my boyfriend beat me and **I don't know where** *to go.*
search terms: social services, shelter, case worker.

John F. Kennedy is my father and I'm routinely abducted by aliens; in fact, some of the accomplices of the aliens are here, among us, in this library. Shall I point them out to you?
Library of Congress Subject Heading: United States—Mental Illness—Popular Works.

From his wheelchair, the paraplegic says: *I want a training course for bounty hunters.*

'You mean for bail bondsmen?'

Exactly. In order to show you the most relevant results

Four searches: five results for western rodeo, fourteen porn sites, six for cheap vacations

we have omitted some entries

two for home remedies (apply directly to the forehead) and one result in kanji.

very similar to the 28 already displayed

Narration is the second lie. The **first is the story** it describes.

His name is Jack,
but you will not call him that.
Jack is his father.

Her name is Rain,
but you will not call her that
or anything.

Because **you do not know** it.
Because you did not ask.

The clocks at your location
are different
and that is because
you are different.

Are crops friendly
to their state of ripeness?
(biologists might call this condition 'happiness')

In the sky
is the future of water, **as it takes shape**
our minds speak back to
whom is speaking,
your hand the sign
of your true age and what you've endured

(I say 'endured' because it's past).

All of our sentences for today
will include one of the following words:
maybe, perhaps or possibly.

We shall not want
    as we walk, we
    as we are when we
walk through the valley of the, the shadow of the
valley palls
our usual assurance—we shall not
want, but we will walk, as people without creed,
we will outlast, we will walk (we've been training)
maybe soonday, **through the shadow of all**
                                        possibly,
as we move through it and out again,
perhaps we can meet for coffee, and while doing it,
maybe we can talk.

The sounds
of weight shifting

are discrete
sounds

forming the equation
of weight shifting.

In The Hopes.

This is a place: The Hopes.

He lacks the language
usual to such things,   but he jumps
                           and flaps and

                        places air beneath him.

For her,
the plant is a different kind of flying: one where you
                           stay still and the world goes by.

Humans (another species
that has forgotten flight
                        and thinks this forgetting fated)

call this inertia,
    believe it is law.

Humans blame it on the rain (which is not a
                        woman's name
                           (because you did not ask,
                              you will not call her that,
                                    or anything,
                                       besides).

You will run but
you will not reach. You will run
some more
and there will be thunderstorms.

For the moment, your reliable agent,
your 'most trusted emissary,'
(which should say something about how
hard it is to get good help [or work, if you can get
it])

These Lilliputians agree with Swift
that tiny cables will be that much more
and if I must
describe, I will be
as scathing as minutiae allows.

You make like you'll drink it, **but you won't**,
Socrates.

Rim of mug to lip of mouth, there is a process
occurring.

Like a train at night, it is metaphor for something
you'll **miss, something**
   that takes from sleep
            and replaces a single memory
                  of all its departures.

When you say you want two,
is it a pay-me-now AND pay-me-later
sort of proposition?

    But you're never quite paid up
    because the world's full of triggers.

'I have a habit of burning bridges while I'm still
                          standing on them.'—Dave Hickey

If only I **could make you
smile that way**,
the way a burning bridge does
just before it
tumbles into the water
that would extinguish it,
everything would be deferred.

We have it all on videotape:
him at the bar, saying how, the **plotting,**
the memory (which stands in for pictures),
just like in the old novel by the young author who
died.

He says Japan, but this is Nihon
where Roland Barthes is selling frankfurters
on an underground level of Shinjuku.

He is walking off in the same body as before,
even though it is differently accessorized.

In a moment, he will come calling; in a second, he'll
come asking after.

They liked the sentiment without liking the point.

Don't tell him where you're going—just go.

The website says, "You have entered the Navajo
Notion."

The Local's Special and the Tourist's Special are
exactly the same price on the menu.

My surname is worth 41 Scrabble points.

That's **what we call ethnicity**.

SYMPTOMS: a small lump where ear meets skull
(I'm trying not to **worry), recurring** twitch in right
bicep, bloodshot eyes even when sober, periods of
anal retention followed by periods of anal expulsion,
blurred vision, swollen lymph nodes, periods of
prolonged grinning when I'm not pleased,
discolored mucus, blood in stool, grinding of teeth,
erections lasting longer than four hours.

DIAGNOSIS: self as pathology.

There are things we will not do
in favor of things
we will not do instead.

This existence **we wilt,**
  growing rapid before blinks have captured
the exact nature of
  our censure of ourselves.

This is why marriage; this is why institution.
This is why,
  night after morning.

We live, as Mamet relates,
  only a few minutes per year.

This will not be one of those moments
when you, free of me, become something
you might have been,

a pronoun free of the syntax
which is summarized *husband.*

And I of you, though I know not
  which part of you I would flee first.

The Penis & The Gravy Boat

Sometimes **you need**
  another year's experience like a turtle needs
                                    a seatbelt.
Sometimes you need some time
    to know what you sometimes need. Sometimes,
you don't think Gertrude Stein is very interesting.
Sometimes, you need a comma
with your sometimes. Sometimes you're at the end
of your rope and you keep climbing. Sometimes
you can't be bothered to consider
what others sometimes need. Sometimes you need
something that you really just want. Sometimes a
simian, rising on his hinds. Sometimes, and;
sometimes or. Sometimes the page will not display.
Sometimes your curiosity is mistaken
for a willingness to purchase.

Sometimes a penis; sometimes a gravy boat.

Coming down the stretch are Charlotte's Web, Jameson Irish, Bangor Maine and The Deputy Administrator. All will place, **none will win**.

The glass is neither half-empty **nor half-full: the glass** is an illusion.

The glass is linguistic description in the act of evaporating.

There are numbers assigned.
I have one.

There is the word *emergency*, but no further instructions.

(This is where context is crucial).

It's called 'slogging.'

Look down: it's what you're doing
in all your life's extremities.

The nouns are coming fast
  and thick, like debris
in a tornado.

You mistake my silence
for a status of 'delayed in publication,'
but copies of this title
are already in stores.

The panic when
it's ten minutes till the closing bell
and you realize you haven't covered your losses.

Everyone's halfway to the bar (going to Carolina in
                                        my mind)
and that's the trouble with genius, no?

Bush vs. Bush. He's not competing with Islam; he's
competing with Dada.

Seven ingredients plus one curse word means I
burned the frittata.

And a damned dull blade it was, too.

I'm going to assassinate you in Second Life and bury
your avatar in **unincorporated** cyberspace.

Do you think we'll ever get around to having that
talk?

But your credit score is our new church, for lack of
something worse, we'll take what you can offer.

The life cycle of certain alphabets is not so brief as
the rhetoric mobilized to hasten their extinction.

'Not' is the 'no **outlet' through which pedestrians** have worn a footpath.

As images replace words
        as the day laborers of interpersonal
communication, we will
right of use, we will catalogue
        for access,
           we use users usually.

Post Scriptum (after RC)

We are nearing the end of another year
    faster than nostalgia's ability to colonize it.

Used to, we'd drive past
  mile marker 78, just to see 79.

But now, we want to get there without the driving.

No ritual exists **for this end time, for the
passenger.**

We haven't far to go now.

When we reach the end, the song has concatenated

       and gives forthwith
something to which we cling,
an expression, an anecdote,

nothing so sure as purchase

     and nothing less than 'home.'

Chris Pusateri is a flyover poet based in Denver. A former resident of London, Mexico City, and Kingston (Jamaica), his accent is a mess. He is the author of several books and chapbooks of poetry, most recently *Molecularity* (Dusie, 2012) and *Anon* (BlazeVox, 2008), and his work appears in many periodicals, including *American Letters & Commentary*, *Boston Review, Chicago Review, Jacket* and *Verse*. A librarian by trade, he lives with his partner, the poet Michelle Naka Pierce.

~ Try another title from Steerage Press ~

Joe Amato, *Big Man with a Shovel*

11597011R00067

Made in the USA
Charleston, SC
08 March 2012